How to Write & Publish Your Book

<u>Now</u>!!

Rachel -
Share your story
with the world!

How to Write & Publish Your Book <u>Now</u>!!

By:
Erika Gilchrist

Published By:
Unstoppable Publishing
13553 South Cicero Ave #176
Crestwood, IL. 60445
866-443-6769

Edited By:
Owen James Parker
owenp9061@gmail.com

Other Books in the Unstoppable Woman's Library:

The Unstoppable Woman's Guide
to Emotional Well-Being

$19.95

The Secrets to Being
an Unstoppable Woman

$19.95

Starting Today

$11.95

10 Ways to Prevent Failure
(Audio Book)

$12.95

ACKNOWLEDGEMENTS

I am taking this opportunity to thank those who have inspired me to be a better me. Owen Parker, my big brother, biggest fan, and strongest supporter, has never once allowed me to doubt just how much of a difference that one person can make, and truly pushes me to raise the bar. I thank you for your unconditional support of my efforts (even the crazy ones). Zernul R. Shackelford Jr., Dr. Anthony L. Gantt, Owen Parker - I thank you all for your insightfulness, creativity, and inspiration that's always "right on time." You all have shown me doors to open that I didn't know existed...thank you.

To my strong circle of friends and family who have never left my side, and has always seen the "light" for me, I am eternally grateful. It is with your encouragement, that I press forward.

INTRODUCTION

"Why me?" This is a question that many people ask themselves repeatedly when it comes to writing a book. The general thought process is that you have to be some sort of guru in order to write a book. This cannot be further from the truth. The real truth is that anyone can write a book, if they so desire. This book is designed to answer the nagging questions that you've had, but perhaps have never asked. At the completion of this book, you will be armed with all the tools, resources, and knowledge you will ever need to write and publish your own book.

One thing this book cannot do is make you start writing. That choice will always be yours. But regardless of when that choice is made, you will be ready. Each person has a story, life-lesson, or significant message, and the world needs to hear it. So instead of asking, "Why me?" you should be asking yourself, "Why _not_ me?"

TABLE OF CONTENTS

1   At Square One – Getting Started................... 11

2   Choosing a Topic....................................15

3   Establish the Purpose of Your Book.............21

4   Selecting a Title for Your Book....................25

5   Gathering Information for Your Book...........31

6   Organizing Your Book..............................37

7   Editing Your Book...................................43

8   Cover Design..51

9   Copyrighting & ISBN...............................55

10 Self Publishing.......................................59

11 Marketing Your Book...............................65

12 Earn Money with Your Book.....................73

CHAPTER 1

At Square One – Getting Started

This is probably one of the most frustrating stages because of all the details associated with writing a book. You have so many thoughts, ideas, and directions and you're not sure how to sort through them all. But the good news is that you have likely already started.

If you have ever journaled your thoughts, or talked to someone about your experiences, then the process has already begun. If you review your journal, would you see some interesting stories that would appeal to people? Has anyone you talked to ever been captivated by the personal experiences that you've had? Then you have started that book writing process!

What's important to remember here is that your goal should never be perfection. Your goal should only be truth. If you start to write for the sake of writing, then your book will not likely impact the lives of others. Your words will be glared over as people browse through the pages seeking some type of emotional or mental stimulation. You don't want to earn a reputation of being a "fluff" writer who only publishes books that don't offer anything real.

A Bad English Student

If you're someone who believes that you're not equipped to be an author because your grammar and spelling is quite frankly, dreadful, then it can be a challenge just to muster enough courage to write a single sentence. You may have daunting memories of teachers telling you how bad your writing is. But the good news (there's always good news) is that there are people on this earth who absolutely live for correcting those types of errors. They're called editors. Remember, your job is not to make the book perfect, it's simply to tell your personal truth. So forget about all of the typos and incorrect sentence structures. Just start writing!

Even if that thought scares you, there's another alternative. Instead of writing, you can simply speak into a microphone and record your thoughts as they come. When you have nothing left to say, you can have your recording transcribed. If you talk a lot, then you should write a lot! This method produces some of the most raw and impactful books because you're speaking from a place undisturbed by technicalities. Your only focus is the message itself.

Another influential element to start writing is to think about all of the people your book will impact. You have something to say and the world needs to hear it. Don't deprive the world of your message any longer. Consider how affected you were when reading some of your favorite books. Think of the emotional triggers, inspiration, vivid stories and deep thought provoking ideals that shook you to your core. Wouldn't it be wonderful to impact others that way?

Be Prepared

Have you ever had a great idea and later on you forgot what it was? You never know when an idea will hit you, or when you'll be inspired to write, so have a pen and notepad readily available. I remember when I was writing my first book, I had Post-It® notes everywhere! I will get into organizing your thoughts later in the book. In the meantime, start writing thoughts down!

> *"Words, when well chosen, have so great a force in them, that a description often gives us more lively ideas than the sight of things themselves."*
> - Joseph Addison

CHAPTER 2

Choosing a Topic

For some people, this may be the easiest part of the book writing process. Some folks have been talking about a particular subject matter for years and it comes naturally to them. They're fascinated by it and can't stop talking about it. Ironically, selecting a topic may be the most difficult part of the writing process for others.

Myths

For some reason, you may have it in your head that in order to write about a particular topic, you have to be some type of certified, world-renowned, master guru in that area. This is not the case. However, you do want to be at least knowledgeable in an area before

15

you choose to write about it. You'll find that the more you write about it, the more research you'll conduct, and the better your understanding will be about the subject.

Another myth about choosing a topic is that you have to choose only one. I know how to cook, and I also know how to drive a car. Who says I can't write a book about them both? Perhaps you enjoy gardening, and you have a fondness for sports cars. Don't limit yourself to a single topic if you are experienced in more than one area.

Start with What You Know

I believe that when you're selecting a topic, you should choose the one(s) that you can stand before a group of people and talk about for hours. There are two elements you should consider when deciding what to write about:

1. **Commitment to Research:** Although you may be very knowledgeable in an area, there may

be some industry changes or trends that will offer your readers more value.

2. **Have a Passion to Share It:** You'll discover that when you genuinely want to share the information, it will flow more naturally and it can actually make book writing a form of release for you.

If you're still unsure about what you should write about, consider this: The best lessons are learned through **experience**. Have you experienced anything that you could share with others? Answer the following questions:

1. Have you ever been through a divorce or bad break-up?
2. Do you work long hours and are still able to get tasks done?
3. Are you a technology fan?
4. Do you enjoy public speaking?
5. Can you repair household things?
6. Are you the "go-to" person for your friends' problems?

17

These are just a few (of millions) experiences that are book worthy. I remember I hosted a roundtable discussion about relationships, and about three hours into it, I discovered that there were at least 25 books that could be written based on the conversation. When I brought the topic up, many of them, like you, didn't think they knew enough about anything to write a whole book about it. After dispelling the myths, they revealed that they were able to write about these topics:

Donald*: I can write about how to be an active father in your child's life, even though you're divorced.

Kathy*: I can teach people how to work full-time from home and make a six-figure income.

Robert*: I can make sense of confusing tax forms during tax season.

Pete*: I can show you how to paint your home like a professional without spending a fortune.

Barbara*: I can write about how to save money at the grocery store utilizing extreme couponing.

Ashley*: I can show people how to travel across the world, and pay less than 50% off retail for their trip.

David*: I can teach people how to create a six-course meal for the holidays for under $100.

Athena*: I can teach people how to make their home more "green."

Vivian*: I can create a cook book filled with old family recipes.

Brian*: I can teach ex-offenders how to become gainfully employed.

The list goes on and on. Do you see what's happening here? These people are no different from you, and after just a brief discussion about writing a book, they were able to hone-in on things they could write about! A common thread in these topics is that they all stem from **experiences**.

Donald can teach others based on his **personal** experience as a single father. Robert can write a book based on his experiences at **work** as a tax consultant. Ashley can teach others about spending less for travel based on her experiences doing what she enjoys **(hobbies)**. Do you see a pattern here?

19

If I were to ask your close friends and family what it is that you're good at, what would they tell me?

_____

_____

_____

_____

Allow your experiences (good or bad) to help prevent others from making excessive mistakes.

> *"Anyone can learn something useful from someone with experience."*
>
> *- Al Capp*

CHAPTER 3

Establish the Purpose of Your Book

When you have numerous thoughts going on, it's easy for your book to stray into different directions. Your readers should always be able to follow the "flow" of your book. In this chapter we're going to cover how to determine the purpose of your book, as well as choosing the type of book you want to write. Let's start with determining the purpose. So here are some things you can do to organize your thoughts so that you can establish the intention of your book:

<u>First</u> – Create a mission statement for your book. This is a single sentence that defines the purpose of your book. To form your statement, ask yourself what you want your readers to "get" from reading your book. For example, the mission statement for this book is:

"To teach people step by step how to get started in writing, organizing and publishing their own book." For my last book, *The Secrets to Being an Unstoppable Woman,* the mission statement was: *"This book will teach women practical techniques that they can implement right away on how to make desirable improvements in their lives through interactive exercises, self reflection, and relatable stories."* Take a moment and think about the purpose of your book and create your mission statement.

Second – Once the mission statement has been produced, start writing from that place. Refer back to it when you get lost. If you start writing and you're not sure if it "fits," ask yourself if it serves the mission of the book. Thoughts don't go in a straight line, so you'll likely start to wander off in your writing process. But this is not a bad thing. When you see your writing starting to drift, don't discard the material...that's another book! Although those thoughts don't fit the current book you're writing, they can easily suit another book you may want to write in the future. Many authors write multiple books simultaneously without realizing it.

Third – Decide who it is you're writing for. Who is your audience? If you're writing about how to resolve health issues, your audience would be those who have health ailments, those who want to prevent them, and those who are caring for others who have them. Write with your audience in mind.

Choose the Type of Book You Will Write

I remember asking someone what type of book they wanted to write, and they responded with, "The kind people read." I thought it was a joke at first, until I saw the sincerity in his eyes and realized he genuinely didn't understand my question. So I recognized it as an opportunity for learning. So I will clarify what it means to choose the type of book you wish to write. There are several types of books:

1. Book of poetry
2. Book of short stories

3. Fiction
4. Non-fiction
5. Self help
6. Cookbook
7. Manual
8. Instruction guide
9. Text book
10. Prayer book
11. Comedic book
12. Illustrative book
13. Children's book
14. Comic book
15. Quote book

This list likely covers the type of book you wish to write. I specialize in self help books because that's my area of expertise. However, I have also written children's stories and short stories. You don't have to limit yourself to one type of book, but be sure that you don't combine them into a single book.

CHAPTER 4

Selecting a Title for Your Book

This is one of the most prominent but underestimated elements of your book. The title and subtitle of your book is what causes people to pull it off of the book shelf over the others. It's what is going to get internet surfers to click on your book instead of the thousands of others they have to choose from.

Your title is generally shorter than your subtitle. The title offers intrigue, and the subtitle offers a more detailed account of the purpose of the book.

I remember watching television and a movie trailer came on. It was starring Samuel L. Jackson and the name of the movie was "Snakes on a Plane." The title of the movie coupled with the trailer let me know exactly what that movie was about. Your mind doesn't wonder what it's about because it's literally stated in the title.

Some key elements to consider when choosing a title are:

1.   Easy to remember

2.   Impactful

3.   Straight to the point

Now there are some titles that do not contain subtitles because the purpose of the book is plainly stated in the title. Having a subtitle to further clarify the book would seem redundant.

Here are some great examples of titles **and** their subtitles:

"The Secrets to Being an Unstoppable Woman" - How to roll up your sleeves, make no excuses, and get what you want! (Erika Gilchrist)

"Attorney Responsibilities & Client Rights" – Your Legal Guide to the Attorney-Client Relationship (Suzan Herkowitz Singer)

"Edgar Cayce's Keys to Health" – Simple Solutions for a Lifetime of Vitality (Eric Mein, M.D.)

"Power" – Why some people have it and others don't (Jeffrey Pfeffer)

Here are some examples of book titles that **do not** contain subtitles:

"Take Control of People in 3 Weeks or Less" - (James K. Van Fleet)

"How to Analyze People on Sight" - (Elsie Lincoln Benedict)

"100 Ways to Create Wealth" - (Steve Chandler)

It wouldn't be fair to offer these great titles without giving you some examples that I have encountered that do not work very well. Some titles that I have seen that do <u>not</u> contain subtitles were:

"Fairy Dust"

"Totally Drained"

"An Inch Away from It All"

27

"Satin Drapes in My Hall"

These titles offer the reader no information about its content. You are left to wonder what the book is about. Now, these titles are just fine if they were accompanied with a more detailed subtitle to provide the reader with more information. So let's pretend they each had subtitles (I'm making these subtitles up):

"Fairy Dust" – A tale of a young girl who believed all the make-believe stories she was ever told

"Totally Drained" – The plumbers guide to fixing every household piping issue

"An Inch Away from It All" – How one man learned to dream big after his battle with a terminal illness

"Satin Drapes in My Hall" – The homeowners guide to spicing up small spaces

Do you see how the titles now have meaning? You can read the subtitles and ascertain whether the subject matter is of interest to you.

28

So now that you're familiar with the basic concept of titling your book, let's get you started. One way is to brainstorm. Write down any and all ideas that come to mind. The purpose isn't to make all of them great, but to get the creative juices flowing. Even if you think the title stinks, write it down anyway. Try to come up with about 10 titles (and subtitles if necessary). The ones that you absolutely hate, toss them. Narrow it down to the ones you like best.

Now it's time to include the people who inspire and support you. Provide them with your list of favorites and be open to receiving feedback. But only survey those who you believe genuinely have a desire to see you succeed. Ask them to be totally honest with you; don't provide colorful comments for the sake of saving your feelings. Ask them if it's a title that would make them pull it off the shelf, or click on it on the internet.

Also, go online and review other titles in your subject matter. See how they're worded; see if they "jump out" at you, or if they have no impact at all. Use this as a guidepost for yourself. You may want to edit two titles to create a single title for yourself.

It's important to know that because there are literally millions of books, you currently cannot copyright the title of your book. So don't be discouraged if you feel you have created the perfect title, only to find it on Amazon or Barnes & Noble.

Your title should be something you're proud of. It should feel good to announce it to others. If you are not satisfied with your title, you will find yourself making excuses for it. If someone asks you the name of your book, and after you tell them you say, "I know the title doesn't sound very good, but the book is solid," or "If you just read the book, you'll figure out why I gave it that title," you may lose that reader.

CHAPTER 5

Gathering Information for Your Book

This is where you add value to your book. The research you conduct will give your readers authenticity and will bring the story or message "home."

Because I specialize is self help books, I like to include real stories, statistics, and practical exercises so my readers will get a better picture of the message I'm trying to convey.

Writers are artists and in general we are very sensitive about our art (words). It's important to us to have our account of the book well received by the readers. Research is where you can hit a home run.

I don't recommend doing research for the sake of research. What I mean is that if you simply start researching without any direction, you lose valuable time. There are a number of strategies in doing research:

> Focus on the current direction of the book and research only that portion.
> Pinpointing particular stats that you know you'll need and save them for when you need them.
> If you're writing a fiction novel, visit the place you're writing about and interview the local people.
> Figure out what you need to know about a topic before you start writing about it.

A common error writers make in gathering information is doing too much research in the beginning and end up tossing much of it. This is why it's important, for the sake of time, to research the information that you know you will need so your book will not frustrate you. This is called *strategic research*.

Where You Should Do Research

We are fortunate to be living in the age of technology. Because of this, we literally have the world's information at our fingertips. "Google" is now a verb. Ask it practically anything and receive hundreds of thousands of responses.

Knowing what other books have been written on your topic is crucial. Review those books and determine what's going to be unique about yours. You certainly don't want to regurgitate the exact ideas as someone else. Remember, writers are artists and we want our own special "flare" to the materials.

Some online research options include:
  ➢   Google or Bing your subject matter
  ➢   Start a blog on the topic
  ➢   Comment on someone else's blog
  ➢   Start a chat about it

➢ Start a discussion on Facebook

➢ Invite opinions of others on LinkedIn

➢ Research similar books on Amazon.com and utilize their "Look Inside!" option, which allows you to read some pages for free.

➢ Join an email list from companies that specialize in your area of interest

Online resources are terrific, and they offer instant gratification and should give you a running start. But there are other research options that provide a more in-depth perspective and there's just no substitute for them.

Some <u>in-person</u> research options include:

➢ Good ole fashioned librarian

➢ Attend a seminar on the topic

➢ Volunteer for a function that surrounds your topic

➢ Host a roundtable discussion

➢ Visit the places of interest

➢ Interview key people who can offer a unique perspective

➢ Reading magazines and newspapers

Don't underestimate the power of research. When you're stuck, do research!

"Care enough about your readers to offer them value. When you do this, they will purchase every book you write thereafter."

- Erika Gilchrist

CHAPTER 6

Organizing Your Book

If you're anything like me, you have spiral notebooks, legal pads, and Post It® notes all over the place filled with tidbits of information that you hopefully plan to use at some point. Perhaps you were inspired and just started writing about a particular thing, or you saw a movie or television commercial and had an idea that you had to write down so you wouldn't forget it. Or you possibly wrote down a dream you had the night before, not knowing if it was going to mean anything later. All of these are great to do, but it leaves you feeling a bit overwhelmed when it comes to putting them in order.

But don't fear! Remember that mission statement you created? That's the best place to start in organizing your thoughts.

Start with an Outline

This provides you with a guidepost to see if you're on the right track. I recommend that you write your mission statement in bold at the top of your outline to refer to it whenever you are having difficulties. Here's an example:

This book will teach people step-by-step how to drive a car one city block.

    I.   Get in the car and do a safety check
        a. Adjust the seat so that it's comfortable
        b. Adjust your rear view and side mirrors
        c. Secure your seatbelt
    II.   Start the car
        a. Allow the car to warm up if necessary
    III.   How to prepare to drive
        a. Apply the brakes
        b. Shift the gear to "D" while still applying the brakes

      c. Check all of your mirrors as well as look over your shoulders to ensure that it's safe to pull away from the curb

      d. Turn the wheel in the direction in which you'd like to go

IV. Start driving

      a. Slowly pull your foot off of the brake (the vehicle will start to move forward)

      b. Adjust the steering wheel to lead the car in the direction you want it to go.

V. Stop the car

      a. Approximately 500 feet before you reach a full city block, apply the brakes to slow down the car

      b. When you reach the end of the block, fully press the brakes to bring the car to a complete stop

This is a pretty elementary example, but it does illustrate the idea of an outline for your book.

The Vision Board

What I have discovered, is that I am a very visual person, so it helps for me to have something I can look at to organize my thoughts. I created a vision board for my book "The Secrets to Being an Unstoppable Woman" and it helps tremendously in putting things in an order that makes sense to the reader. I first took a large poster board and divided it into large sections. Each section is labeled a specific chapter. I then wrote on sticky notes and placed them under the appropriate heading. I even color coded it to further organize my thoughts.

For example, the orange sticky notes represented a story I wanted to tell, the green ones were for statistics, and blue ones were for thoughts I had on that topic. On the next page is an example of a vision board on how to make a pie:

The great thing about using sticky notes, is that you can remove them from one section and place them in another with little or no effort. Talk about organizing!

When you are able to organize your book, it becomes much easier to write, and more importantly, it becomes much easier to read.

\-   Erika Gilchrist

CHAPTER 7

Editing Your Book

After you have written your book, it is essential to have it properly edited. I stress the word "properly" because not all editors are treated equally.

If you are a fiction writer telling a story with a setting in African American culture, it helps tremendously to have an editor who is familiar with it. If you fancy writing about wild animals, it would behoove you to have an editor who can distinguish the varying species of those animals and have the resources to do fact checking about them.

All editing isn't created equal. There are various types of editing and it's important that you are able to distinguish the difference so that you'll know which type of editor you will need.

The first time I sat down with an editor, she asked me, "What type of editing do you want me to do?" I wasn't aware at the time of varying degrees of editing. I thought it was all the same. I admitted my lack of knowledge in this area, and she was very kind in explaining it to me. She told me that some writers are very good, so there's very little editing that needs to be done. She went on to explain that sometimes writers are very bad at sentence structure, organizing thoughts, and word usage, so it would require more extensive types of editing.

I really appreciated her patience with me as I was learning about becoming a published author. Five books later, I am very familiar with the editing process.

I will break this up into four stages of editing -

Content Editing (also called developmental or substantive editing) is the first stage. This is to ensure that the book has an organized "flow" and is easy for the reader to understand. This content edit will ensure that the subject matter is clear and that the ideas are clearly written and focused. This type of editing will separate a professional book from an amateur book. Some of the things that will occur during a content edit:

➤ Identifying and solving problems of overall clarity and accuracy (fact checking)

➤ Reorganizing paragraphs, chapters and sentences to create a more readable flow

➤ A market analysis

➤ Writing and rewriting of content

➤ Adding new material to fill in the gaps as well as deleting old material that doesn't work

➤ Ensuring that the book follows a logical sequence

➤ Making sure that the author's thoughts and focus are coherent and well written

The next type of edit is called **copy editing** (also called line editing). This stage consists of focusing on the grammar, punctuation, spelling and sentence structure. Think of copy editing as your elementary school English teacher going through your book with a red pen to correct your grammar. This section includes:

➢ Breaking up run-on sentences

➢ Reducing overused words

➢ Ensuring correct word usage (whose vs. who's)

➢ Noting permissions needed to publish copyrighted material

➢ Clarifying the meaning of the work and improving readability

➢ Reducing paragraphs that are too long and choppy

The next stage of editing would be the **design edit** (also called layout, or interior design). Many people combine this stage with the copy edit and it's perfectly acceptable. I wanted to separate it here so you will be perfectly clear about how many details are involved in creating a professional and polished manuscript. The design editor covers:

> The typesetting

> Page margins

> Placement of illustrations, charts, graphs

> Chapter headings and subheadings are aligned properly

> Adding or removing bold, italics, and underlining that doesn't work

> Making sure that the book is appealing to the eye and the layout doesn't confuse the reader

Lastly, the manuscript goes through **proofreading**. This is where the smallest of the "fine tooth combs" are used in identifying possible errors. It can include:

> The final copy is read to check for errors that the writer and other editor(s) may have missed

> Reading for flow without checking the previously edited copy

➤ Ensuring that all of the changes have been incorporated

When selecting an editor, ask him/her which type of editing is their area of expertise. This is a crucial step in producing a quality product. Some authors choose to do a self-edit, which is common, but not the best option. It's better to have an objective person to read your words to determine how the message is actually coming across to the readers. You need someone else to say, "Did you really mean to say it this way?" or "I noticed that these paragraphs are not in sequential order."

The smallest details can easily be overlooked. Read this aloud:

> # HOUSES ON THE THE HILL

You read, "Houses on the hill, right?" Look again. It states "Houses on ***THE THE*** hill."

Here are some resources that you may consider when searching for an editor:

- ➤ www.Guru.com

- ➤ www.Elance.com

- ➤ www.ProofReadingPal.com

Online searches will provide hundreds more. But I have had great experiences with the resources listed above.

One thing a writer doesn't want to overlook is good editing. After months of researching and crafting a piece, you don't want your readers preoccupied with errors and inconsistencies. It's worth the time and money.

"Not having an editor is like having a great movie script with very bad actors."

- Erika Gilchrist

CHAPTER 8

Cover Design

We all know the old saying, "You can't judge a book by its cover," but the fact is that it's exactly what people do when browsing through books. An appealing cover will draw the eyes of the reader. You want the cover of your book to harmonize the inside pages. The graphic designer's work is seen long before the readers get to the impeccable work of the editor.

When selecting a graphic designer, ask for samples of their work. Be sure to ask if they have ever created a book cover. Some designers target logo design, or t-shirts, or web design.

If you're not a graphic designer, I strongly recommend hiring a professional instead of trying to do it yourself. There's nothing worse than having a solid, substantial manuscript with a cover that is clearly shoddy and amateurish.

Your designer will need to know the specifications or "specs" of the book. That means he/she will need to know the size of the book, the number of pages, the size of the spine, bleed areas and more.

Your cover should invite your readers to open the book. It should be the focal point of the piece. If your book is sitting on a shelf with other books, the spine will be the only thing people see, so keep that in mind when designing the cover.

Don't get too "artsy-fartsy" with your cover. There was an author who asked for my opinion on her book cover. She had the picture of the Statue of Liberty on the cover with various names of U.S. cities floating around it. Her book was about gun control. I was thinking, "What part of this cover says gun control?!" She must have read my facial expression, because the next thing she said was, "I believe that in America, freedom and opportunity is granted to us from coast to coast, but not if it's going to endanger the lives of its citizens."

She was going for the symbolism as opposed to making it clear. The issue is that her target audience won't likely pick up her book because they will perceive it a completely different way!

Granted, there will be numerous opinions about a single book cover, but let the debate be about color, size, or appeal. Don't let the argument be "What the heck is this book about?"

When I conceptualized the cover of this book, I wanted to show the book writing process. So I explained it to my graphic designer and this is the final product. Sure, I could have used other fonts, colors, and sizes, but the circle graph is clearly in alignment with the book's purpose.

Will everyone be happy with your cover design? Absolutely not! But it's important that *you* are happy with it.

"When it comes to book covers,
there is no single

right answer."

- Erika Gilchrist

CHAPTER 9

Copyrighting & ISBN

For someone who is not detailed oriented, this portion of the process can simply be mind numbing.

Copyrighting

First let's be clear about what this is. Copyrighting is an exclusive legal right given to the originator of work. This means that the work that you produce legally belongs to you. It can be a painting, book, poem, illustration, song, a film or other types of work. Basically anything that you originate can be copyrighted (except for book titles as we covered earlier in the book). There are certain rights that come along with being the lawful creator of said works. Some of them include:

➤ Reproduction of the work

➤ The ability to dispute copies and/or sue

> ➢ The ability to display the work publicly

You want to copyright your book to protect you from having your work stolen by another who can claim it as their own. So how do you do that?

The Copyrighting Process

To properly copyright your material, you should first go to the U.S. Copyright Office online:
www.copyright.gov

Here you can start the process. It walks you through a series of questions about your book such as the number of pages, other contributing authors, the type of manuscript, and many other factors. You can also upload your work, or mail it in. The current fee for copyrighting your book (authorship) online is $35. This is a very small price to pay to protect all the time and effort you have put forth in writing your book.

There has been another form of "copyright" that many people have used. They would mail themselves a copy of their work and when receiving it, they keep it sealed without opening it, using the postage date as proof of when the work was produced. This is often called the "poor man's copyright." My opinion about this process is simple. We spend far more than $35 on things we simply don't need. Why not spend it to protect yourself? Things happen and if your mailing happens to get lost, stolen, or damaged you are basically screwed.

ISBN

The International Standard Book Number is a thirteen digit number (formally ten digits) assigned to every book for the recording of the details of the book such as title and publisher. This is how bookstores and online book sellers identify your book.

Do you need an ISBN to self publish? No, you don't. You can self publish your book and sell them out of the trunk of your car and it's perfectly legal. But for the purposes of selling through bookstores, libraries, and wholesalers (distribution), you must have an ISBN assigned to your book.

It's possible to self publish your book and add an ISBN to it later.

How to Get an ISBN

The most common place to obtain an ISBN is through the U.S. Identifiers Agency – Bowker:

www.myidentifiers.com

You will be prompted to enter details of your book so you can be assigned a number. Currently, the price for a single ISBN is $125. Or, you can buy a bulk of them for discounted rates. For example, for ten (10) ISBNs, you pay $250 (only $25 each). This is a very desirable option if you plan to write multiple books.

Buying an ISBN improves the chances your book will be found online or through other search methods.

CHAPTER 10

Self Publishing

So now you have a completed manuscript in your hands and you want to bring it to life. Self publishing is basically defined as: *The publication of any book or other media by the author of the work, without the involvement of an established third-party publisher.*

I want to focus on that last part, "...without the involvement of an established third-party publisher." I highly recommend self publishing for a number of reasons.

First, long gone are the days of slaving over a manuscript and pitching it to large publishers in hopes that they will see the value that you see in your book. Self publishing allows you to say to the big publishers, "Hey! I don't need you to validate my work." You can publish it yourself and start getting exposure now. You can pitch it to a large publisher later.

Did you know that the best-selling book *Rich Dad Poor Dad* by Robert Kiyosaki was originally a self published book before it was picked up commercially?

More benefits of self publishing are:

➢ You have complete control over all aspects of your book including design, marketing, distribution, size, and price point.

➢ You receive all revenues from the sales of your book.

➢ You retain the rights to all of your work.

➢ You may do whatever you wish with your books – give them away, discount them, sell them, change them…anything.

How to Choose a Printing Company

As a self publisher, it's imperative that you use a reputable and professional printing company to print your books. If you do an online search on book printing companies, you will be bombarded with pages of companies. My suggestion when contacting them is to ask for book samples. Many printing companies will send you a sample book that they have printed to showcase the quality of work they produce. But don't be fooled either. In most cases, they will send you the highest quality book which means that the book has been printed on the most expensive paper and cover stock, it's been designed by a professional graphic designer and has undergone several stages of editing. Indeed many printing companies are a "one stop shop," but don't believe that your book will turn out as great as the sample if you choose their less expensive options.

Here are some more things to consider when choosing a printing company:

➤ If you can upload your own cover, or if you have to use their in-house designers

➤ The turnaround time

➤ If there's a live person you can speak with

- If they offer packages within your budget

- If they can mail you a physical proof before it's printed (bounded, not loose leaf)

- What the payment terms are

You may have to print the same book with different printing companies before you find one that you really like (another benefit of being self published). Also ask other authors who they choose to do their printing.

Some printing companies offer to sell you an ISBN for a much cheaper rate than Bowker (as low as $55). But be mindful, that if you choose that option, you will no longer be the publisher of that book, they will. And they will be the main contact for your book.

How Pricing is Determined

Most printing companies will have a pricing calculator that will help you to stay within your budget. The standard minimum for ordering books is 25. However, I have seen companies that go as low as 10. Here's the information you will need to know in order to determine how much your books will cost you to print:

- ➤ Size of the book (6 X9, 5.5 X 8.5)

- ➤ Number of pages

- ➤ Type of paper

- ➤ Number of interior color pages

- ➤ Number of copies

- ➤ Binding type (perfect bound, coil, saddle stitch, hard cover, paperback)

- ➤ Where it's being shipped to

The smaller the order, the higher 'per book' price you're going to pay. If you want to make a profit with your book, it's best to order in higher quantities. For example, if your book is 200 pages, and the retail price is $15, if you only order 25 books, it may cost you $12 per book to print. So your profit margin is extremely small. But if you order 500 books, you may only pay $5 per book.

What Do You Want from Them?

Determine what it is you are looking for in a printer. Do you want them to simply print what you have as is, or do you want them to design the cover, edit the manuscript, or market and distribute your book? These services are very convenient when they're centralized. If you don't have the energy to seek out individual editors, graphic designers, and marketers, this may be a desirable option for you.

Do Your Research

Read reviews of these printing companies to see if you can determine a common thread, both positive and negative. If a company has a reputation for being fast, but the quality is bad, you may want to go with someone else. You've worked too hard on your book to let it get to this stage and choose an inferior company.

Self publishing can be very rewarding, but there's a lot more work involved. The success (and failure) of your book solely rests on your shoulders. It also requires on-going investment funds.

CHAPTER 11

Marketing Your Book

To prevent having a basement or garage full of your books, let's look at how we can get them to move. This is done through marketing.

This topic is so vast, that there's no way I can squeeze everything into a single chapter. I will, however, provide you with some tools you can use to get you started on the right track.

Pre-Marketing Plan

Believe it or not, much of the marketing is done prior to the publication of the book. You want to create a buzz with your book and doing so beforehand is the key.

I highly recommend the book *1001 Ways to Market Your Books* by John Kremer. This book is over 700 pages and can seem overwhelming, but it's an invaluable tool to assist you in every aspect of book marketing.

In the meantime, I will provide you with some strategies that I have found to be effective.

1. Book Fact Sheet – Create a fact sheet about the book. Include the who, what, when, where, how and why. This is to make it easier for media to understand what the book is about.

2. Choose the best media outlet – Decide what type of media you want to expose your book to. Newspapers, radio, television, magazines, online media…etc, and make sure their readers/viewers are in alignment with your target audience.

3. Find expert endorsements – If you're able to leverage any relationships, solicit known experts in your field to write a positive testimonial for your book. Or even better, have them write the foreword.

4. Join a Book Club – You can do this in person, online, or both. Get to know how the group functions so you'll know how to present your book to them.

5. Create a media kit – You want to have a professional representation of your book. Include your bio, other books you have written, any articles that you've been featured in, shows you have appeared on, clubs, groups and organizations you're part of, and anything that might be of interest to the media.

6. Secure a following online – Create a Facebook Fan Page for the book and direct people to "like" your page. Announce it on LinkedIn, and have your Twitter followers tell their friends to follow you.

7. Pre-Sell the book – Offer the book for sale before its publication date. This money will help cover the costs you incur in marketing your book yourself. You may choose to offer it at a discounted rate as an incentive.

The Launch

1. Press Releases – Have a professional write a dynamite press release highlighting the benefits of your book. Be sure to have them include hyperlinks of keywords so it's easily located when doing an online search. Send the press release out to targeted media more than once. Resend it every two weeks and follow up with the media outlets.

2. Schedule interviews – Call local shows and tie your book into current events. For example, if it's near Valentine's Day, you may want to pitch your book if it was about romance and relationships. Having a book about women's issues may be great around breast cancer awareness month.

3. Give it away – Send review copies to radio and television producers along with your media kit and follow up a week after it has been delivered.

4. Book Signings – You may choose to do a local book tour, or a major release party. Go crazy with the media invitations. Completely saturate your local media with the announcement and host it at a venue that will give the appearance of a packed house. For example, if you're expecting 75 people to attend, you don't want to book a hall whose capacity is 500, because it will look like you had a poor turnout. Don't let the room "swallow" your guests. An intimate, classy venue will do just fine.

5. Create a video – Have a professional create a 30-60 second commercial for your book and saturate the internet via social media, YouTube, and other video outlets. Be sure to use keywords that will guide viewers to your video. You may also want to play this video at your book signing repeatedly (looped).

6. Leverage relationships – Does someone owe you a favor? Is someone willing to do you a favor? Great! Ask them to connect you with

their contacts who can assist you in your venture. Ask not, have not!

7. Be part of a trade show – This option can be rather expensive, but depending on your budget, it can certainly be worth it. You may want to consider splitting the cost with another entrepreneur whose business compliments yours.

8. Attend the BookExpo America (BEA) – This event happens once a year and it's the largest publishing event in North America. Each event promises to give you access to what's new, what's next, and everything exciting in the world of books. To learn more about what's going on at BEA, you can go to their website: www.BookExpoAmerica.com

Get Creative!

Again, there are many ways to market your book and feel free to get very creative. Here are some things I like to do:

➢ Volunteer - One of the things I do is volunteer to help others with their projects. I will call them out of the blue and ask how I can assist them with their next project. They're so grateful that when I ask them to help me, it's always "yes" provided they're not prescheduled. This works in multiple ways. I feel good about helping another person, I meet new people at their event(s), and I now have another person who I can call upon when I need help. Oh, and guess what I bring with me when I volunteer? That's right, my book! I have bookmarks, business cards, postcards and any other marketing materials that I can fit into my briefcase. Opportunity is everywhere.

➢ Stand in long lines – Anyplace where I have to stand in long lines, I bring my book and pretend to read it: The Department of Motor Vehicles, grocery stores, banks, airports, hotel check-in, concert lines, bus stops, and even amusement parks. I even chuckle out loud to get the attention of the others in line. In most cases, people can't resist and ask me what I'm reading and there's my "in."

If there's one piece of advice that I can offer that should stick, it would be to constantly market your book. Don't stop. Be a shameless promoter!

> *"Planning is the first and most crucial step in marketing any book, so be sure you do it justice."*
>
> *- John Kremer*

CHAPTER 12

Earn Money

with Your Book

In this economy, it's important to create multiple streams of income. Having a book gives you more leverage in accomplishing this. We've established that having a book adds credibility and allows people to view you as a subject matter expert. What I have come to understand is that people pay for expertise.

And this doesn't mean that you know any more about a topic than they do. But when you have published a book about it, the perception dramatically changes.

As a speaker, I'm often told that I did a great job, or that I am being recommended to another contact for another speaking engagement. These are wonderful things to hear, but for years, I was a speaker without a product. I traveled across the world delivering powerful keynote speeches, workshops, and trainings…without a book.

One day I attended a seminar and I recall how good it felt to be a participant instead of the educator. I took plenty of notes and absorbed the new information being presented. During the breaks and at the end of the seminar, I noted how many people visited the back table to shop for products written by the presenter. I also perused the selection and my attention was drawn to a statement that I heard the assistant say to another participant, "Your total comes to $136 please." I couldn't help turning my head to see what he had purchased for $136. The assistant handed him two bags with about four books in each bag. I remember thinking, "Hmmm, the seminar didn't even cost that much."

This piqued my curiosity like you wouldn't believe! I became nearly obsessed with finding out how many more people were going to make purchases. I watched that back table like a hawk. And by my calculations, there had to be more than $1,000 in sales from the books alone. It was like someone snapped me out of a trance. How could I have missed such a golden opportunity? I quickly tried to assess how many speaking engagements I had done up until that point, and when I did the math, it felt like the air left my lungs. I had been speaking for years, and by my calculations, I left at least $100,000 on the table that I will never be able to regain. Talk about a wakeup call!

So, my friends, I beseech you to understand the leverage you have in being a published author. I implore you to utilize these techniques to earn money with your book:

> ➢ Book speaking engagements – Not all speakers are authors, and not all authors are speakers. But if you have a book about a particular subject matter, start doing speaking engagements about it. You can start by doing the speaking engagement for free, provided you're allowed to sell your book(s) there. Even if you have just 30 people in the room, you have the potential of earning over $500 from the "back of the room" sales. Pitch your book

from the podium. Talk about bullet points your audience will find in the book. You may say something like, "Today I'm going to cover two ways to cure acne, but my book offers five ways." As you're doing your speech, have the physical book in your hand and turn the pages as if you're taking information directly from it. Don't read from the book, but what happens is that subliminally, your audience will think, "I have to have that book to find out more!" You may also include the price of the book in the ticket sales and pitch "workshop includes a copy of the book."

➢ Get referrals – When you do speaking engagements for free (which is very easy to do), ask your contact person to refer you to more contacts who would be willing to book you as a speaker. Repeat the same routine as before. Eventually, you'll be able to charge a nominal fee for your time in addition to selling your books.

➤ Write multiple books – You might be thinking, "Are you crazy? It was hard enough to write just one Erika!" This may be so, but what I have found is that once you write your first book, the others are easier to write. When you have multiple books, you can offer packages. For example, I have six books in my library that retail for $100. I can offer all six at a discounted rate of $75. The person may only have an interest in one or two, but when you offer discounts, they can think of people to gift the others to.

➤ Create a coaching program – If people are willing to attend a seminar, or buy your book about its topic, they will be willing to be coached on it one on one. A perfect example of this is the book you're holding in your hands. I offer a 30 day coaching program designed to help people write a book in 30 days. If you write about how to lose weight, create a coaching program for your clients/readers so

77

they can have you all to themselves for their personalized weight loss goals.

➢ Sell to colleges and universities – If your topic is of a technical nature, you may want to consider selling to institutions that have a special interest in it. If your book is about "Knock Out Presentation Skills" you may want to pitch your book to a school that offers an entrepreneurship program.

➢ Pre sell your book – Before it's actually released, offer it at a discounted rate for a limited time.

➢ Sell it online – Completely saturate social media with your book's presence. You may choose to offer it at 20% for a particular season, or special occasion. Around Valentine's Day, I offer discounts one week prior on my books focused on women's emotional wellness. Get interviewed on numerous blogs mentioning your book, and get booked on online radio shows.

➤ Bookstore sales – This is a very old trick, but it still works. Have a group of your friends and family call local bookstores asking if they carry your title. Of course the book store will say 'no' but after so many inquiries, they will eventually seek out your book. This is one of the reasons why it's important to have an ISBN for your book. In order for this to work, don't overdo it. Don't ask everyone to call all on the same day. Bookstore owners are aware that this is likely a ploy. You want to "drip" your way into the stores. I think a good measuring stick would be four calls per week for a month. Then walk into the bookstore with copies in your hand, and ask for the store owner. Set up a book signing and be prepared to provide how you plan to market your book to drive sales in the bookstore.

➤ Bulk sales – Pitch your book to a related company asking them to purchase your book in bulk. For example, if you write a book about financial responsibility, contact banks to pitch

79

offering your book as an incentive for opening a new account. They can purchase hundreds (or thousands) of them and give them away to new customers. You may also pitch this to large trade shows. Wouldn't it be great if their website read, "Complimentary book with each ticket sale!" knowing it was *your* book?

➢ Spontaneously – A true professional always has copies of his/her book within a moment's reach. Even if you have them in the trunk of your car, that's fine. As long as you can say, "Yes, I have some that you can purchase right now," that's great. Remember standing in line at the grocery store? What if the customer standing behind you wants to buy one right then? Would you be prepared to sell one?

So where do you go from here? Anywhere you want to. You no longer have to sell your book in traditional ways. Keep track of what works for you and repeat it. Then, write a book about it!

About the Author

 Erika Gilchrist, *"The Unstoppable Woman,"* is regarded as one of the most energizing, engaging, and captivating speakers in the industry. A partial list of corporations, associations and universities that have attended Erika's speaking engagements include:

- Monster (.com)
- Enterprise Rent A Car
- Mississippi Valley State University

Erika is a Chicago native and during her youth, she has witnessed firsthand the effects that gang violence, drug abuse and poverty has had on her community. As a result, she developed a strong passion for empowering people to overcome barriers to make them unstoppable in their own lives. Despite challenging surroundings during her formative years, Erika has achieved great success:

- 2007 Highest Trainer Rating of the Year
- Self published author of eight (8) books
- Trained more than 5,000 people on how to become self published authors
- Former on-air radio personality on WKKC 89.3 FM Chicago

83

Book Erika to Speak at Your Next Event!

Name: _____

Title: _____

Company: _____

Email: _____

Website: _____

Phone: _____

Event: _____

_____

Complete this preliminary information and send it to:

Erika Gilchrist Enterprises

13353 South Cicero Ave #176

Crestwood, IL. 60445

Or email to: info@erikagilchrist.com

www.ErikaGilchrist.com

Bring This Workshop to Your Club, Group or Organization!

Now that you have read the book, if you need more information, or a personalized class, Ms. Gilchrist would be happy to come to your organization to conduct a workshop for you. Contact us today for more detailed information. Let's get you started right away in becoming a published author! **Call Now: 866-443-6769**

Psst! Are you a little confused and need help? I'm at your service! Call me to coach you privately so you can be on the fast track to being a published author:

866-443-6769 ext 2
info@erikagilchrist.com

"If and when my name becomes valuable, I have to mention this workshop and this woman. She is clear, she keeps it simple, and covers all concerns in realistic detail."

- *Jonathan P.*

"What I liked the most about this workshop was the capability of actually starting the writing process, and having the opportunity to talk with people who have been down this road before."

- *Delvin R.*

"My confidence was over the top, and I have Erika to thank for it! She challenged me to dig deeper, get more creative, and really send a message."

- *Deborah C.*

"If you've been thinking about writing a book, and you don't know where to start, Erika will be there every step of the way to guide and encourage you."

- *Suzanne L.*

Made in the USA
San Bernardino, CA
03 April 2016